Farm Machines
at Work

Skid Steers
Go to Work

Emma Carlson Berne

Lerner Publications ◆ Minneapolis

To Bruce Gaskins, for patiently explaining the finer points of farm equipment and for answering many phone calls

New Holland is a registered trademark of CNH International and is used under license.

Lerner Publications Company
A division of Lerner Publishing Group, Inc.
241 First Avenue North
Minneapolis, MN 55401 USA

For reading levels and more information, look up this title at www.lernerbooks.com.

Main body text set in Billy Infant Semibold 17/23.
Typeface provided by SparkyType.

Library of Congress Cataloging-in-Publication Data

Names: Berne, Emma Carlson, author.
Title: Skid steers go to work / Emma Carlson Berne.
Description: Minneapolis : Lerner Publications, 2018. | Series: Farm machines at work | Includes
    bibliographical references and index.
Identifiers: LCCN 2017050333 (print) | LCCN 2017051674 (ebook) | ISBN 9781541526082 (eb pdf) |
    ISBN 9781541526044 (lb : alk. paper) | ISBN 9781541527690 (pb : alk. paper)
Subjects: LCSH: Agricultural machinery—Juvenile literature. | Loaders (Machines)—Juvenile literature.
Classification: LCC S675.25 (ebook) | LCC S675.25 .B47 2018 (print) | DDC 631.3—dc23

LC record available at https://lccn.loc.gov/2017050333

Manufactured in the United States of America
1-44584-35503-3/28/2018

TABLE OF CONTENTS

1
FARMS NEED
SKID STEERS

A skid steer does a lot of work on a farm. It looks like a mini bulldozer.

NEW HOLLAND L216

Sometimes farmers need to move logs around on their land.

Farmers use skid steers to lift and move heavy things. Skid steers can lift logs, bales of hay, or grain.

Skid steers can plow snow or move and dump dirt. Sometimes people use skid steers on construction sites too.

Every skid steer has a cab. Two arms reach out in front of the skid steer's cab.

Usually a bucket is between the two arms.
The bucket can scoop things up.

A skid steer's bucket can come off. Farmers sometimes put other tools on the skid steer instead. They can attach a special tool to help hold round bales of hay.

Different tools make it possible for a skid steer to do special jobs.

Another tool on the skid steer can help plant a tree. This attachment is a tree spade.

A tree spade can dig a hole for a tree and then plant the tree.

A farmer sits inside the skid steer's cab. There are levers and pedals that control the skid steer. The farmer can raise and lower the arms and the bucket from the cab. She can also drive the skid steer.

NEW HOLLAND

Tracks help a skid steer grip the slippery ground.

The skid steer has two wheels on each side. A farmer can replace the wheels with tracks. The tracks help the skid steer grip the ground on dirt or in snow.

Skid steers are useful on a farm all year long. Farmers often use skid steers in the fall to lift big bales of hay.

The skid steer can also be used in the winter. The skid steer can shovel snow.

The bucket tool scoops up snow in the winter.

Some farmers use skid steers to feed cows. The cows line up. The skid steer dumps grain in their troughs.

SKID STEERS YESTERDAY, TODAY, AND TOMORROW

Two brothers named Cyril and Louis Keller invented an early skid steer to help a farmer move manure.

The Keller brothers worked on a turkey farm.

Then a farm company thought that other farmers might like this new machine. They started making many skid steers.

Soon skid steers were being used for more things.

Skid steers are still very popular on farms. They can do many different jobs, and they are easy to drive.

Companies are always looking for ways to make skid steers better. Some new skid steers can lift even more weight than before. Jobs are a little easier for farmers because of skid steers.

SKID STEER PARTS

cab

bucket

L 218

NEW HOLLAND

200 SERIES

arm

tire

20

FUN SKID STEER FACTS

- Early skid steers had one wheel at the back and a wheel on each side. Newer skid steers have two wheels on each side.

- Besides lifting hay bales, many farmers use the bucket on skid steers to scoop and dump manure.

- Farmers can attach giant brooms to the front of their skid steers. The brooms can sweep up dirt and rocks on a road.

GLOSSARY

attach: to put two pieces together. An attachment is a part that is put on a machine.

cab: the area in a vehicle where the driver sits

lever: a bar for moving or steering something

manure: the waste of animals like horses, cows, turkeys, or sheep

pedal: a bar at foot level to move or steer something

trough: a long, narrow, open container that animals eat out of

FURTHER READING

Boothroyd, Jennifer. *Tractors Go to Work*. Minneapolis: Lerner Publications, 2019.

Dufek, Holly. *A Year on the Farm*. Austin, TX: Octane, 2015.

"Tractor Video (for Kids)—REAL Farm Tractors"
https://www.youtube.com/watch?v=o1yvsxAmiZY

USDA for Kids
https://www.usda.gov/our-agency/initiatives/usda-kids

Walendorf, Kurt. *Hooray for Farmers!* Minneapolis: Lerner Publications, 2017.

Weingarten, E. T. *Tractors*. New York: Gareth Stevens, 2016.

EXPLORE MORE

Learn even more about skid steers! Scan the QR code to see photos and videos of skid steers in action.

INDEX

PHOTO ACKNOWLEDGMENTS

The images in this book are used with the permission of New Holland except: Sunny Forest/Shutterstock.com, p. 16 (background); Bearok/Shutterstock.com, p. 16 (turkey inset); Laura Westlund/Independent Picture Service, p. 23 (tractor). Design elements: enjoynz/DigitalVision Vectors/Getty Images; CHEMADAN/Shutterstock.com; pingebat/Shutterstock.com; LongQuattro/Shutterstock.com.

Cover: New Holland.